KU-351-195

THE
Little Book
— OF —
MIRACLES

This book is dedicated to all my friends
and Mighty Companions who choose
The Way of The Happy Dream,
The Way of Miracles.

MIRACLES

THE
Little Book
— OF —
MIRACLES
Quotations from *A Course in Miracles*

compiled by

HEBE TAYLOR

ELEMENT
Shaftesbury, Dorset ♦ Rockport, Massachusetts
Brisbane, Queensland

References to A Course In Miracles
are marked with section letters and page numbers by the quotations.
The letter T means Text, W means Workbook, M means Manual, L means Lesson.
All quotations are taken from the new edition unless marked 'O'.

First published in Great Britain in 1995 by
ELEMENT BOOKS LIMITED
Shaftesbury, Dorset

Published in the USA in 1995 by
ELEMENT, INC.
42 Broadway, Rockport, MA 01966

Published in Australia in 1995 by
ELEMENT BOOKS LIMITED
for JACARANDA WILEY LIMITED
33 Park Road, Milton, Brisbane, 4064

Designed and created by:
The Bridgewater Book Company / Ron Bryant-Funnell
Photographs by Hebe Taylor and Sarah Bentley
Cover photo by Steve Satufhek / The Image Bank
Background tints by The Telegraph Colour Library
Printed and bound in Hong Kong

British Library Cataloguing in Publication data available

Library of Congress Cataloging in Publication data available

ISBN 1-85230-618-1

Extracts from *A Course in Miracles* ® © 1975, reprinted by permission of
the Foundation For Inner Peace Inc.,
P.O. Box 1104, Glen Ellen, CA 95442, USA.
A Course in Miracles is published in the UK by Penguin/Arkana Books

Introduction

Welcome to THE LITTLE BOOK OF MIRACLES. It is a companion to a much bigger book: *A Course in Miracles*.

It started one cold dark winter's day in 1986. I felt different and could not explain it.

I lay inert for most of the day, not doing anything. Then a miracle occurred. At around 4pm my right arm, as if it did not belong to me, reached over and picked up a thick paperback book with a green cover and gold writing. This large volume had lain unopened and forgotten on the bedside table on the right of my bed, where I keep books waiting to be read. It had been waiting for me for a long time. It was *A Course in Miracles*. It fell open at page 362, Chapter 18 and I read the subtitle:

I need do nothing

It described perfectly the process I had entered into that day. I felt a thrill as I read: *To do nothing is to rest, and make a place within you where the activity of the body ceases to demand attention…*

Isn't this what I had done, or not done, all day?

…This quiet centre in which you do nothing, will remain with you, giving you rest in the midst of every busy doing on which you are sent.

I could not stop reading *A Course in Miracles* once I had begun. I wanted to carry it around with me wherever and whenever possible. This was not always practical, it being a large volume of over one thousand pages.

So, I began writing down on small pieces of paper my favourite passages from the big book, as these were much easier to carry around with me. I was often greatly moved by the beauty of the words I read, and being a visual person I could also see images that corresponded with the words.

I began recording my favourite quotations in a small hardback notebook my brother had given me, and to add pictures from my own photographs. Sometimes I would purposely go out and photograph my impression of the quotation.

A book began to grow with words and images. It became such a good companion that I wanted to share it. Friends said they would like a copy and that it should be published.

So here it is.

I shall not describe *A Course in Miracles* because I think it speaks for itself. If by reading this book you are drawn to discover the treasure house from which these excerpts were chosen, it will be the second step you have taken towards a more miraculous life. And so I joyfully share with you this LITTLE BOOK OF MIRACLES.

With love,
HEBE

*P*REPARE

yourself

for

miracles

today.

W190
L106

———✦———

NOTHING can

hurt you

unless you

give it the

power to

do so.

T 432

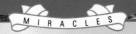

...SEEK not to
change
the world, but
choose
to change
your mind about
the world.

T445

A MIRACLE is never
lost. It may touch
many people you
have not even met,
and produce
undreamed of
changes in
situations of which
you are not even
aware.

T6

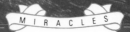
*M*IRACLES arise
from a
miraculous state of mind,
or a state of miracle-
readiness *T6*

*I*N the teaching-
learning situation,
each one learns that
giving and receiving
are the same.

M6

$\mathcal{W}$HO would attempt to
fly with the tiny wings of
a sparrow when the
mighty power of an eagle
has been given him?

M9

You have been given
to your brother that
love might be
extended, not cut off
from him.   *T501*

No one at one with
himself can even
conceive of conflict.

M12

◄ 13 ►

MIRACLES

To give up all problems
to one Answer is to
reverse the thinking of
the world entirely. And
that alone is
faithfulness.

M15

ONLY the open-minded
can be at peace, for
they alone see reason
for it.

M16

IN my
defencelessness my
safety lies.

W284

FOR you will not see the
light, until you offer it to
all your brothers. As they
take it from your hands,
so will you recognize it as
your own.

W285

*N*o longer
is the
world our
enemy, for
we have
chosen that
we be its
Friend.

W371

STEP back
from fear, and
make advance
to love.

W 376

*I*LLUSION

makes illusion.

Except one.

Forgiveness is

illusion that is

W379

answer to the

rest.

Forgive the past
and let it go, for
it *IS* gone.

T552

In everyone you
see but the
reflection of what
you choose to have
him be to you.

T528

*I*N you is all of
heaven. Every leaf
that falls is given life
in you. Each bird that
ever sang will sing
again in you.
And every flower
that ever bloomed
has saved its perfume
and its loveliness
for you.

7527

$\mathcal{F}$ORGIVENESS is
the great
release from
time. It is the
key to learning
that the past
is over.

7551

*N*o accident nor
chance is possible
within the universe as
God created it, outside
of which is nothing.

T448

*T*HE miracle is
possible when cause
and consequence are
brought together, not
kept separate.

T557

And all you need
to do is but to wish
that Heaven be
given you instead
of hell, and every
bolt and barrier

T546

that seems to hold
the door securely
barred and locked
will merely fall
away and
disappear.

BE not content
with future
happiness. It
has no meaning,
and is not your
just reward. For
you have cause
for freedom
NOW.

T560

FORGIVENESS removes
only the untrue, lifting
the shadows from the
world and carrying it,
safe and sure within its
gentleness, to the bright
world of new and clean
perception.

T396

———

LOVE is not learned,
because there never was
a time in which you
knew it not.

T396

... *Separation* is but
empty space,
enclosing nothing,
doing nothing, and as
unsubstantial as the
empty place between
the ripples that a
ship has made in
passing by.

T597

Be not afraid, but let
your world be lit by
miracles.

OT555

BE willing, for an
instant, to leave your
altars free of what you
placed upon them, and
what is really there you
T449   cannot fail to see.

THE holy instant is not
an instant of creation,
but of recognition. For
recognition comes of
vision and suspended
judgement.   T450

*A*LL that is
asked of you is to
make room for
 truth.

*I*T is but the
first few steps along
the right way that
seem hard, for you have
chosen, although you
still may think you can
go back and make the
other choice. This is
not so. A choice made
with the power of
Heaven to uphold
it cannot be
undone...

T477

... *Y*OUR way is
decided. There will
be nothing you will
not be told, if you
T477   acknowledge this.

A JOURNEY from
yourself does   T655
not exist.

*T*HERE are no accidents...those who are to meet will meet...they are ready for each other.

M7

---

*T*HE blood of hatred fades to let the grass grow green again, and let the flowers be all white and sparkling in the summer sun.

T561

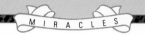
For what would seem
to need a thousand
years can easily be done
in just one instant by
the grace of God.

W374

Your judgement has
been lifted from the
world by your
decision for a happy
day.

T629

$\mathcal{T}$HE trumpets of
eternity resound
throughout the
stillness, yet disturb it
not. *7592*

A CLOUD does
not put out the
sun.

T620

✛

*T*HE memory of
God is shimmering
across the wide
horizons of our
minds.

W399

*I*F you have no
investment in anything in
this world, you can teach
the poor where their
treasure is. *T220*

*R*ECOGNIZE *WHAT DOES NOT
MATTER*, and if your
brothers ask you for
something 'outrageous',
do it *BECAUSE* it
does not matter.

T221

THE morning star
of this new day
looks on a
different world...

M92

THE stillness and the
peace of *NOW* enfold
you in perfect
gentleness.

T349

*L*OOK not to idols.
Do not seek outside
yourself. *T618*

---

*T*HE journey to God is
merely the reawakening of
the knowledge of where you
are always, and what you
are forever. It is a journey
without distance to a goal
that has never changed.

T150

*W*HAT God has
willed for you *IS*
yours. He has
given His Will to
T150 His treasure,
whose treasure it
is. Your heart lies
where your
treasure is, as His
does.

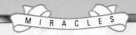

*W*HEN you meet anyone,
remember it is a holy
encounter. As you see him
you will see yourself. As
you treat him you will treat
yourself. As you think of
him you will think of
yourself. Never forget this,
for in him you will find
yourself or lose yourself.

*M*Y thoughts
do not mean
anything.

*T*o recognize this
is to recognize
nothingness when
you think you see
it. As such, it is
the prerequisite
for vision.

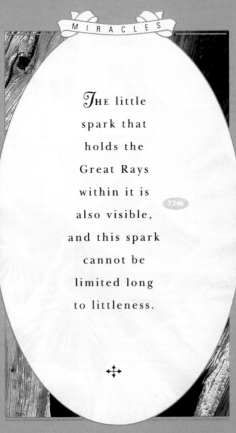

THE little
spark that
holds the
Great Rays
within it is
also visible,
and this spark
cannot be
limited long
to littleness.

T-346

*E*ACH lily of forgiveness
offers all the world the
silent miracle of love.

W473

---

*Y*OUR passage through
time and space is not at
random. You cannot but
be in the right place at
the right time. Such is
the strength of God.
Such are His gifts.

W65

DREAM softly of your
sinless brother, who
unites with you in holy
innocence.

T585

THE miracle comes quietly
into the mind that stops an
instant and is still.

T591

THE miracle but shows
the past is gone, and
what has truly gone has
no effects.

T589

THIS world is full of
miracles. They stand in
shining silence next to
every dream of pain and
suffering, of sin and
guilt.

T595

... *Y*OU have barely started
to allow your first,
uncertain steps to be
directed up the ladder
separation led you down.
The miracle alone is your
concern at present.

T396

*G*OD builds the bridge, but
only in the space left clean
and vacant by the miracle.

T397

*H*EALING is the effect
of minds that join, as
sickness comes from
minds that separate.

T596

*W*HAT is forgiveness?
Forgiveness recognizes
what you thought your
brother did to you has
not occurred.

W401

I REST in
God.

W197

I AM
entitled to
miracles.

W137

ACKNOWLEDGEMENTS

Robert Skutch at the Foundation for Inner Peace for granting me permission to quote from *A Course in Miracles*.

Arkana for issuing the licence.

David Wood (The First) for being my wonderful friend and guide and for introducing me to so many wonderful ideas, not least *A Course in Miracles*, and for doing the word processing.

My wonderful Mother, **Ruth**, aged 95 years, who still attends occasional meetings of the Course in Miracles group and who has so generously contributed to my life in so many ways, including supplying me with the cameras I use for my photographic work.

And likewise my brothers, **David** and **Stanley**, and my **Father**.

And all my friends and Mighty Companions for their love and encouragement including: Jeffrey, Mary Ann, Silvia, Judith M., Judith C., Sam W., Sam K., Simon, Nik, Melanie, James Karen and Joshua, Ron, Zana, Ian, Salvador, J.B., Rebekah, Kate, Mohan, Lynne and Dwight, Lori, Laurie, James M, Sue, David and Clifford, Katrina, Mother Meera, Dimitri and David Wood (The Second) for his trust, support and generosity, and Ian Patrick, Robert and Miranda Holden and Max Dowling of the A.C.I.M. network.

Thanks to **Sarah Thiel** who sent me the NEW EDITION of *A Course in Miracles*.

And last, but not least, **Ian Fenton** for editorial suggestions.

And of course, **ELEMENT BOOKS**.

Seminars and workshops:

The Actors Institute	Insight Seminars
Werner Erhard	Shaun DeWarren
Marianne Williamson	The Life Training
Chuck Spezzano	MoneyLove
Clare Clearlight	Michael Portelly
Sondra Rae	Kew Gardens - course in
Betty Palko	photography and for being a place
Kenneth and Gloria Wapnick	of great beauty and inspiration.

Hebe Taylor is a multi-talented entertainer, singing teacher, writer and photographer. She leads groups in *A Course in Miracles*, which she has studied for ten years.

Cover photo: Steve Satufhek/The Image Bank. Background tints: The Telegraph Colour Library. Additional photography by Sarah Bentley.